Ethereal Echoes: Poems of Love, Soul and Life

Ila Sharma

BookLeaf Publishing

India | USA | UK

Presentation by *BookLeaf Publishing*

Web: www.bookleafpub.com

E-mail: info@bookleafpub.com

ISBN - 9789363315372

First edition 2024

ACKNOWLEDGEMENT

I offer my deepest gratitude to God, whose divine guidance and grace have illuminated my path and blessed me with the gift of words. To my beloved Mommy and Papa, whose unconditional love, unwavering support and belief in my dreams have been my pillars of strength throughout this journey, I am forever indebted. Special thanks to my sister, Anshu, whose inspiration fuels my creativity and passion. To my brother Aalok, your encouragement has always been a beacon of strength. To my husband, Rahul Dev, thank you for your endless support and belief in me. To my dear friends and students, who unknowingly motivate and inspire me with their enthusiasm and curiosity, I am forever grateful. Thank you all for being the pillars of my journey in art and poetry.

PREFACE

In the pages of this book, you will find a collection of poems that I have penned over the years, each born from moments of introspection, moments of connection with the world around me and moments of profound emotion. These poems are my attempt to capture the essence of life, love and the human soul and to offer readers a glimpse into the beauty and complexity of existence. I hope that within these verses, you will find echoes of your own experiences and emotions and that they will resonate with you in ways that are both meaningful and transformative.

The Power Within Me

It was a knock at the door,
The sound was breaking the silence.
I was confused by my mind's sudden roar,
As the knock was from self-reliance.

Happiness was the guest with a proffer,
My mind was lured by the pleasant offer,
as it was a moment of relief,
To free myself from demolished belief.

Now I'm over with the pangs of jaundiced mind,
To prove my worth to the world that's blind.
As the beauty of peace comes from within,
And the power of independence is ready to
begin.

The opinion of folks can't define my value.
My today's visitor was standing with a clue.
The applauding thought comes with bliss,
Giving my psyche a moment of peace.
Now I'm breaking my mind's insidious chains
To enhance my value sans musing about the
world again.

Flow of Thoughts

It was an aesthetic day.
Nature was swinging in a polychromic way
The vibgyor colors dancing on the rope
And the soothing air flowing through the hill
slopes,
The view outside the window was mesmerizing,
But inside a gentle pain was stirring.

Every little pore in the air,
Was generating a strange flare.
The mind mania was demanding a direction
with the terminal correction.
It's stupefying how it flies
Leaving a distraction to arise.

Sometimes from pleasure to pain
trying to pass through a narrow lane.
Suddenly a raindrop broke the silence
helping me to fight that inner violence.
Nature was showing mercy with little droplets
and knitting the scattered thoughts in couplets,
Providing a chilling effect on the mind and soul
I got a glimpse of peace's bowl.
The serenity of the mother nature
was appearing as a preacher

And inspiring every pore in the atmosphere.
To bind the thoughts without any fear,
The sweet aroma was still on the way
Uplifting the high spirit like a shining ray.

In the Dark

It was a moonless night,
But still, my way had a sparkling light.
A stormy rain was about to start,
And lifting sparks in my heart.
Moving alone on that scary path,
Was just like measuring the crematorium's
depth.

Initiating gloom in front of my eyes,
That dingy night was boosting the fear to rise.
Reaching the horizon was the ultimate decision,
So amity with the dusky night was the
conclusion.
Then little pearls provide a soothing touch to my
sight
And enlightened my soul to make the way
bright.

Going ahead in the silvery flare,
Was enough to crush my inner fear.
Further movement was cutting the edge of the
night's horror
And made my way with a twinkling glitter.
Who says darkness just ensnares pain?
It relies upon us to get nectar from rain.

Peep of the day was ready with the dawn chorus,
And now I could touch the horizon's colors.

Meeting with an Angel

Life gave me a chance to meet an angel,
Compiling those thoughts here isn't a doodle.
A cushy feeling encouraged me to indite that
And made my life joyful and pleasant.
Someone read the pain in my eyes,
Which was there because of the world's lies
And gradually made a place in my heart.
So, I owe my happiness to that part.

As pain and pleasure walk hand in hand,
He became my personal heroine brand.
Admiration turned into an unconditional
sensation
And became a cause of an everlasting
impression.
I guess that ardor emotion was mutual,
But prolonging it with an angel wasn't possible.
He wished to add charm with a cheery touch,
But time flew away because of a loose clutch.
Fear of losing him ensnared the mind,
Proving true that love is blind.

He was gone leaving everything behind,
Knitting threads of life with gold strings.
Meeting him again doesn't look feasible,

The path shown by him is achievable.
I feel blessed upon meeting with an angel.
Happiness is in the air changing life's angle.
A little pain is overcome by self-confidence,
Euphoria in my heart could still feel his
presence.

Seeing the Rain, That Night

A bunch of thoughts crossed my mind,
The heart felt it and the eyes cried.
The beautiful memories were throwing some
light
And let the darkness of the night
To allow the thunder to be bright
The roaring sound of lightning
And the clouds were drenching,
Nature was unveiling
The cries, the pain, the sorrows, the fears
As the whole earth was drowning in tears

Wailing for the aid
Wanting for the man to forget this trade
To save the bounties of nature
As we are all its creatures
The tears and the rain moved together
Like a torrent and comforting the weather.

The night was getting better
With every bit of darkness
Just hoping for the day, thereafter,
To bring back its blissfulness.

I am Insane

Looking out of my window,
Under the cloud cover
The gifts of nature,
The buildings of humans,
The sprinkling of rain
And seeing all my efforts going in vain.

I was trying to enjoy the rain,
Moving in hustle-bustle on my train.
Every tree passing by through every lane,
Was telling me that you are insane.

Laughing at the thought that now I have no
brain,
Was giving me goosebumps and a little pain.
My dreams were as big as a crane,
Difficult to infer the colors of methane.

The sound of the river was showing faith in me,
The touch of air was filling new vigor in me,
Encouraging me to loosen the grip of fear and
run
And cheering me up to not refrain
But then the world cried,
"You are Insane."

You are Insane.
And your mind needs to be trained,
The vehicle running to its destination
I just smiled again.

I reached as I was in a mesmerizing chain,
I danced in the rain.
Because I am Insane
I am Insane.

Come Back Again

See! I am dancing in the rain.
It's a hurricane.
Love has come again
In the form of a hurricane
And I am dancing in the rain.
Look! What am I feeling?
Like an insane.
Let's not let it go mundane
Come back again!
Come back again!

Journey of Life

Magical like poetry,
Untouched by touch.
Touch with your eyes and the flow of wind.

Drunk without wine,
Some words are left unsaid...
And the visitor is still waiting,
To cross the lines
For a station that will never come
To begin a journey that will never end
As we are in a different era.

The soul will feel,
While the time will heal
And the station thus reveals
The journey should be carried forward with zeal.

Last Night's Dream

A storm came near me,
First, touched my skin
Then gripped my veins
Now swallowing my arteries
Trying to cease my breath.

It's growing on me
Covering every ounce and length
Ingesting me in its depth
It's slowly growing on me.

Terminating my voice
As if that storm felt rejoice.
My eyes, unready to open
And the storm was going strong without any
weapon.
It was growing on me.

The breathing, about to stop
And the life going off the rope
The dead end seems like the next stop
The soul, still strangled and in mope
Ready to be paralyzed by the storm
Everything was kept mum,
Couldn't stop the cyclone to come
Giving me my voice back.

Suddenly, the wail was ready to crack,
As I got my senses back
And the dream ended
As I laid down on my back.

My Mother

When I opened my eyes to the world,
An embrace of yours felt like a shield
That's when I know it's you! Mother
As God has sent me to the divine creature.

When I cried first,
Your warmth put me in an unknown zest
As I was in a safe crest.
You made me believe in this process of life.
Like you! It's the perfection I strive for.

Values and morals, I imbibed from you
Has always helped me to confront the crew.
I believe in angels, sparks, magic and more
Because I know it's all in you mother.
It's difficult to sum up all that you've done
But your presence makes my world a heaven!

Sea Love

The sunlight adding beauty to the sand
And the sand not giving me the way to land.
Waves crashing on my shore,
The wind touching me to the core
With my last bottle of rum
 I'm waiting for some message to come.

I saw the waves coming to me
Carrying a bottled message,
Like a killing spree!
A hope of getting someone,
On a stranded island
Added more shine to the sand.

I felt my aura with the luminous vibrations
In reliance of getting someone and some ration
The wind blew in the direction of the wild trees
As the caged birds just got free.

The message in the bottle
showed some presence.
It has reached me after covering the oceans.
A man searching for love
On a free weekend

And I searching for someone
On a deserted island.

Find me

I hope you find me there,
Where rivers tinkle with the stones
Although I am not lost.
Just find me on the untravelled path
I am walking on a lost adventure.

Beware! The path can have danger
Not of stones and hurdles,
But of losing the path of the real world.
Find me in the florid sky
As it bears all my passion
Find me in the thin line
That ornates the starry shine.
Find me in the whispers of air.
As you call my name in a sudden flare.

I hope you find me there,
Where waves are touched veraciously,
By the velocity of an airy melody.
I am not hiding my valiant lover!
Just find me
Or I'll find you.
As I am walking on this adventure.

Someone Like You

I was like a broken dream
And then you entered my life as an energetic
beam.
Understanding that's God's will
Was just like a confusing thrill.

Now it was time for the end of an eclipse,
Because I just experienced an angel's glimpse.
It was the time for dawn,
When I got a chance to wear your friendship's
crown.

Feeling blessed with the end of that dusk.
Now you and I are 'We' in life's walk.
There is no reason for my rise (fall) for you
I've always dreamt of a person
Someone Like You.

Art of Living

Every day had a soothing breeze,
But my lips were missing cheeze.
Each moment was full of gloom
And the sight of my mind waiting for it to bloom
Somewhere that euphoric mood was missing,
Spoiling my power of reasoning.

Further moment wasn't feasible in hurly-burly,
Suddenly a divine message touched me gently.
Now the air had mesmerizing effect
Giving my mind and soul a complete rest.
Meditation took me to my inner self
Adding brightness and charm to my life.

Now even I can fly
And feeling the pleasure of getting high.
Healing my life with the technique of breathing
Just wish to pay my gratitude to
Art of Living.

Memories of Love

The ice sheet was enough to set my heart on fire
Every time the snowflake touched my skin
It brought back your memory.

You are in my soul.
You are in my breath.
You are in my smile
You are in my tears
You are in my eyes
You are in my brain

But Listen! My heart gets injured
By the memories' crane,
You are not in my arms.
There are snow-covered sheets
They are on the verge of drought.
My soul is burning.

As it needs the warmth of your touch.
It needs snowflakes to rain.
Again, Again and Again!
Please come back to my heart's empty lane.
I hope our love doesn't go in vain.

Starry Flare

Owing to the embrace of stars with the sky
The little one closed her eyes.
With the unending darkness,
A path was there to spot the starry mess
And the journey begins
To a blissful ride of dreams.

At the end of darken room
A white lily was ready to bloom
And now she was in a different world
Enchanting fragrance and stars curled
Ambience of silver and golden flare.

Every time she moved and uncovered another
layer.
She encountered the sight that was very rare,
Chaotic wind with magnetic ware
She was lost in the serenity of the starry flare.

The chaos, helping her to blossom,
Showing her mind about things she couldn't
fathom.
There was so much more to explore
She was embracing that dark roar.

As she moved further,
The flourishing white lilies were welcoming her.
She embraced the dream and the reality with that
uncovered layer.

Sealed Love

As the chilling breeze touched me gently,
I wish to seal my love for you.
We will not be talking verbally;
We will witness nature's view.

We are not in unison
But the golden string that we are holding
Adds the valor in the surrounding
And leaving the sky to become crimson.

I am holding this serene feeling
With every pore that's healing.
I am breathing my love for you.
I am sealing my love for you.

Passing Moments

The fragrance of the air,
And the aroma of fire,
The stillness of water, I captured,
With the clatter of soil,
People come and go
And I pondered about the moment to stay.

With the smile of tik-tok,
Time just passed away.
Dancing with the bubbles around.
Felt the bliss with every second
People come and go
And I pondered about the moment to stay.

The New Year Time

It was the twilight of the dawn,
That was making the folks yawn.
The passing of time was the main concern
And the murky feelings were crossing the lane.

The beautiful fog was emblazing the brain
Making my inner soul enlightened,
The broken heart was ready to upturn
With the new timeline,
To do something and make myself gladden.

The past will always have some recollection
For the present to move with some lesson
And then the future can have more illumination.
The beauty of thoughts was giving a reflection
To be firm and happy
To follow the resolutions.

Forever

Forever is that felicity
That changes the life's velocity.
Forever is neon,
That we always yearn for.
Forever is a joy,
Containing the heart's chords' alloy.

Forever is not a lie
Because when you fly
You see the different colors of the sky.
Forever is a dream,
As it lets you float in a beautiful stream.
Forever is a luxury,
Where the word 'love' gets its summary.

Forever is a bliss,
Just wish to catch it, before I miss it.
Forever is like a shower,
Where gleeful moments stay
Forever and Forever.

The Unknown Visitor

Magical like poetry,
Untouched by touch,
Touch with your eyes and with the flow of the
wind
Drunk without wine.

Some words, left unsaid and
The visitor still waiting to cross the lines,
For a station that will never come
And the journey will never end
As we are in a different era.

The soul will feel
While time will heal
And the station thus reveals
The journey should be carried forward with zeal.

Go With the Flow

It all starts with a notion
To go with the flow
Or move against the direction
That's when you shouldn't bow.

From summer sunshine to winter wine
Just take up the situation
Enjoying the sight of the horizon
Let it soak you in emotions
Before it all goes.

Let it drench you with the last drop of ocean
Before it gets frozen
Let it save you
Before the time stands in a queue.

So, let's drown in this ocean
And enjoy empathic creations
It all starts with a notion
Let's go with the flow.

Light within Her

She entered into a dangerous state that night
Stars along with the moon,
Shimmer along with the dark,
Bliss along with the blisters
Her dreams along with the agony
Now she was ready to enter the bleak hope
As of now, there was no turning back
It was time to enter lowlights and
turn them into bright lights.

Quest of Life

As the waves unfold their destiny
And hurriedly left for the shore.
They moved as far as they could
With all their strength
Jostled by the moonlight
Trying to part ways
From their benefactor
Trying to outdo their alpha.

In the quest for life beyond the sand
The sea wasn't afraid.
It calmly inhales the moon's reflection
It knew this would pass
For the ballistic waves
Are its innate nerves.

And when the waves reached the shore
The sand parted ways with the water
That's when it pulls down its anger
Moving back to sea
And embraced the ocean under the moonlight
With a blissful delight
And the stars witnessed the groovy night.

The Silent Knight

Under the covers
There lied a little girl
Who has made her pain
As her shield
And she drank her tears.
As she lay down her sword,
With the bleeding letters on the canvas
And her beating heart on the edges
With the silent knight
Sleeping in her soul
It was ready to wake up.

Love's Zest

It all began with a quest,
Not allowing me to rest.
Drawing a bead on the path
This time I will do mental math.

Something drawing me towards you
Your eyes that dagger-like blue,
It sired the love in the air,
Unfolding your mesmerism in each layer
That hankering in the soul,
To decipher your role
And my heart, looking for a bolthole.

The energy kept yanking me on you
I was just moving with no clue.
As the void between us kept filling
The abyss of love turned out enthralling
And all the pain was healing
Making our horizon chromatic
And filling our lives with Aesthetics.

As I take your hand in my hand
I felt the fulfillment of my quest
And I'll capture all this in my wand
Now our love decides to rest.

As to be in my heart like a fest
It's enough for me to zest
It's enough for me to zest.

Beyond The World

There's a place beyond the stars
And I will meet you there soon.
I'm not new to saying this to my lover
But I am like the dew that can alter
The wind's cover.

Don't forget this intensity,
When you go beyond the clouds
As I will wait for you
On the moon
Away from the crowd.
You'll have to find me
On that alien land
In the sea of sand.

Then put your ashes in my wand
I will be there over the moon.
When you'll take my gypsy soul
We then will become whole
And the universe will witness
The togetherness of two loons
There's a place beyond the stars
And I will meet you there soon.

I am a Passerby

I am a passerby,
I'll take energy from the moon,
And I'm ready to swoon.
I'll take energy from the stars
And I'm ready for scars
I'll take energy from the sun
And I'm ready as the nut shun.
I'll take energy from the light
And see how bright it is.
Come, join me!
I am the passerby.

Feel It

I am dust in sand
And I'll dissolve in the air
As the light will touch me
Come along with me.
Let's get lost in this vacuum
Before you become a vacuum.

Soulful Nature

From now don't keep memories in folders
Rather keep them on a patio
Along the bonfire,
With close friends
And the vibrant colors of the sky
As when you will see the colors.

The sky will shout out to the memories,
Closed in the folders of your tablet
Let the soulful nature
Have the soul of your best times.
Let it remind you
The serenity of your memories
So that you don't try hard
To keep it safe in the technological folders.

Let your beautiful memories
Be the air you breathe.
Let the harsh memories
Be the fire you release.

Let the memories of your struggle
Be the water in which you mould.
Let the memories of your success
Be the soil on which you ground.

Let the memories of your existence
Be the clouds in the infinite sky.

Hope

As she was hexed with the Supernova of words,
Moving on her sinuous path
There was a little fear in her moonshot
But with little wolf's bane
In her silhouette,
She managed to unburden
From all energy vampires
Making it free from ardent fires!!

Listen!

Something that will never happen again
That little piece of my heart
That little tenderness in the form of words
That spontaneous love comes from my heart
In that nanosecond,

Did you feel it?

Listen to those words...
And the murmuring continued
At that moment we might feel forever
In that nanosecond, you'll feel it
But words may not continue
Like the morning dew.
But I will be there for you.
Just for you!
Just for you!

Love at First Sight

When I lifted the book,
The air could feel your aroma
And when I opened it
The breathing could feel all the words.
Filling me with your smell
Telling all the shrubs used
It was love at first sight.

Nature's Direction

When the dreams knock
At the mind's door
In the middle of the night
And you get up.

May the moon guide you
May the fireflies lighten your way
And the butterflies in your belly
Brighten up your vision.

Don't let the idea sleep now
As it's taking you to the path
That has channelized your wroth
Into something positive and worth.

Let the moon guide you
And let the fireflies lighten your way
Let the difficulties get away
While you play your part in this world's play.

Serenity of Nature

I saw the cotton weeds
Running through the dark side,
With the purple streaks of clouds.
In that dark night,
The shining armor sprinkled the stars
Into my inside knight.

With the bolt of the thunder
Along the crystalline clouds,
The soil reflected upon the sky
Matching the softness of the soul
With that cotton weed roll
The knight with the armor smiled
And the clouds growled
On the side when the air chiseled

With the subtle murmur effect on the shining
armor
Drowning all the Greys of the thunder
The sky reflected on the soil
With the shining coil
Nature captured the essence of its elements
Leaving a stillness
And spreading some serenity in the turmoil.

Soulmates

With the thunder rumbling
And the bold showers
This time I sniffed you coming
As the soulful air touched me
And the lightning clicked me

This time I felt you coming
As the clouds giggled
And the rain chortled
This time I saw you coming
With all the natural clicks
And when the storm passed

It was all on the cards
As I got you
And you got me.
For wonderful years to surpass.

Shrined Love

I have traveled to faraway places
From the mountains
To the depth of the oceans
From the vast seas
To the natural vegetation
All these have filled my heart with appreciation.

But there is a little empty space
I want to fill it with your embrace
As it yearns for our shine
For our love magnifies as an enshrine
And the universe will see
Our alliance leads to the nines.

The Little Magenta Creature

I saw the waves surfing on the sand
With that little creature on its side
Searching for some viand
Moving along the tide

Beckoned with the waves
She was enjoying the stride
I suppose she got that dulcet bite
For that; her heart craves.

Then the air whistled
And the sky called
That little magenta creature
She was now back to her maven creator
Leaving a little sprinkle on sand, air and water.

Come Out Of It

In the hands of your demons,
When the bad summons
Just put your head up once
Before letting all the good lanced
Come out of it.
Just keep the spirit high
And come out of it
Just come out of it.

Spectrums of Life

In the intensity of the breath
And the freshness of the sparkle
Across the universe
Beneath you
And beyond that is all
There are some verses, that flow
Across the waves.

Where you will find some twinkle,
Somewhere a beautiful stillness
Find a little part of yourself
There, in that very moment

Capture that intensity of your breath
Just regain your strength
And join the life's wavelengths
For new spectrums of life.

Desires

There are things that I want to buy
Maybe to use them,
Maybe just to own them,
I have many of them by now
I will own many of them soon.

Maybe for a thing called desire
That prevails deep in ourselves.
It needs to be taken care of
For the fulfillment of the mind.

But don't take it to the soul.
Keep it away from the desires
For the things you don't want now
For the wishes that don't prevail now.

The body has passed through that
And it will pass through every wish.
Make sure to fulfill it.
Maybe, dissolve it.
For the soul to evolve through it.

We Will Meet Another Day

In the middle of the cosmos,
Before the words turned to prose
It was trying to make sense in the environs
And our first look in the chaos
Sent a signal from the boss.

Though the magic wasn't visible
But the air crossed its way
To make it feasible
And the tables turned with a ray.
The calmness was incredible
Turning the tempo magical.

And the time passed
With the spread of mysterious sprinkle
Leaving its tails to be beheld.
May the air pass through the heart's gateway
And the cosmos digs up its role in the play
Then, we will meet another day
We will meet another day.

It's All Within You

You see all the eyes watching you
Are they really watching?
Or is it just you?
Looking for the answers around you?
What you are looking for
Is inside you.
The seekers that look for the answers,
The thinkers that look for a comeback,
The insanity that looks for the outer world,
Listen to everything around you
It's all within you.
The answers that feel right
The comeback, which is bright
And the world, that is infinite
It's all within you.
All the eyes in the world are ready
To embrace your insanity,
To admire your thoughts
And to present what you seek
It's time to unfold your dimensions.
As it is all within you
It's all within you.

Open Your Soul

Open your soul
To the variants of the universe.
Listen to the sounds of the environment,
Feel the surrounding air,
Smile to the brightness of lightning
And surrender yourself to infinity
That is inside all of us
And you will know about the universe
That inculcates everything that surrounds us.

Be Ready

In the blink of an eye,
When the air will strike away
All your innocence
That's when you will crave it
And the thunder will make you realize
You are a grown-up girl.
Just be ready for the storm
Take charge of its direction
And the rain will guide you.
Just hold up the courage to reach your
destination.

Nature Talks

Whenever you witness
The rumbling of clouds,
Trees dancing on the songs of air,
The sun peeping out of the clouds
And the soft sprinkles of the nature
The lightning clicking your pictures
Listen to all of it.

As the divine is talking to you
Listen to the sounds of clouds,
Dance on the songs of the air,
Have a glance at the sparkling sun
Behind the clouds.

Get yourself wet in the soft sprinkles
That's when nature is talking to you
Just Listen to all of it.
And get yourself lost in earth's serenity pit.

In That Night

In that night
When the moon was hiding behind the clouds,
She waited for him to come
As the stars were ready to shine
Staring at the dark night
As her eyes turned to stones,
She waited for him to come.

The wind turned its direction
And the clouds rumbled.
The sky cried with thunder
As the clouds' tears touched her stone eyes,
She waited for him to come.

Thunders turned into soft hush
And the moon showed up.
The stars gifted their shine to her eyes
And in the blink of eyes
The knight just showed up.

In a way, nobody has imagined.
In the way, old stories were written.
Her wait was over
As if time traveled fast
And all the manifestations came true.

The universe witnessed the union
That night.

It's Your Time

It's high time for you Girl!
That you push your cycles away
And rewrite your destiny.

It's time to break the patterns of the past
And break all the shackles.
Just come out of the blurry vision
Of this world's outdated thoughts.

It's time for you to fly high
You will see the sky roaring in golden colors
Encouraging you!
Supporting you!

It's your time
To embrace your regnant-self
And rewrite your destiny.

Be Your Own self

Listen, girl! They will smile with you.
At some point, they will smile at you.
You are managing to adjust here
In a world full of fake glare.

Folks will like you,
While you adhere to their old blues,
They will show support
When you agree to remain in tort.

They enjoy their lucrative trammel
And accepts you only when you
remain in joy-coated shackles
But you!

Be open with your wild soul
Who will never be ready for a stormy scroll.
Just remember your free self
Which will not settle for noxious elves.

Be Yourself

There will be a time
When your thoughts can become a crime
Witness your explosion of freedom of mind
And see who stays.

Who can bear those fire chunks?
Because you know girl
Those who are bearing the heat of your fire
Deserve to be in your heart's lyre.

Just be in your very self
And witness life creates an ardent shelf
As that is outright
To experience the existence of your real self
That is free and infinite.
So, be that girl!
Just be that!

My Love for You

Windows rustling as the air streams in
The sound of the leaves creaking
And the window points out the view outside.

The wind touched my face gently
As if it was you!
It felt like a rough smile
Juggling to come out from me.

I know it was time
To smile again,
To feel the purity again.
The wind whispered in my ear
As if it was presenting its proposal.

And My Life! I felt you
With closed eyes, I heard you
And I wish the breeze stayed here
And talk more about you.

The wind, the leaves, the windows
And every particle around me
Is having a sense of awareness
That you won't come for caress
My eyes felt it all and the rain flashed the pain.

I felt it all again.

Your love my dear
I hope you are at peace
And our memories would always be treasure
As I felt our love again.

Blissful Life

When the life is mixing new colors,
Opening its arms for fresh covers
And deep inside your mind hovers.
But you keep moving as a good roamer
From far you may not like the rover
As the air passes and you move closer.
The eye gaze makes the process slower
Turning the thoughts clearer,
While breaking the mind's false towers.
Behold the clarity when the bliss showers
That's when the lover in you sees another lover.

Moments

The fragrance of the air
and the aroma of fire
The stillness of the water I captured
With the clatter of soil.

People come and go
And I pondered about the moment to stay
With the smile of tik-tok
Time just passed away.

Dancing with the bubbles around,
Felt the bliss with every second
People come and go
And I pondered about the moment to stay.

Graceful Love

As she gigged out of her window,
Sipping her green tea
A plethora of emotions comes through
As she was diving in the deep sea
Sipping the seaweed colored through purple
skies.

Dealing with her surged feelings
Sounds near the abode turning lows to highs.
It was one moment of that eternal warmth
Sipping the hues with the soothing air.
The velocity of emotion that took her breath
Giving her bliss with the utmost flare.

Engulfed in her emotions sipping the green tea,
Fondness of the feeling made her free
Witnessing the rise of the sun
With another day of unknown yearn.

She comforted the butterflies in her belly
With another sip of her green tea.
Love was all around across the valley
Moving along with a blissful spree.

As she noticed a pathway through the clouds
Where certain things were left unsaid
And ready to join the crowds
Where her mind needs to pretend.

Still engulfed in the beauty of the feeling
As she sipped the last sip of her green tea
Making a way for a strong base.
She carried the love with grace
And she carried the love with grace.

Come Back

Ice sheet enough to set my heart on fire
Every time the snowflake touched my skin it
brought your memories.

You are in my soul.
You are in my breath.
You are in my tears.
You are in my smile.
You are in my eyes.
You are in my brain.

But my heart gets injured by
the memories of crane.
As you are not in my arms
There are snow-covered sheets.

But are on the verge of draught
My soul is burning
As it needs the warmth of your touch.

It needs snowflakes' rain.
Again, again and again!
Please come back to my heart's empty lane.

Soulful Love

In the very moment of eternal drizzling
The air singing and nature's calling
Something was knocking at my mind's door
That I was likely to ignore.

Knock knock knock!
It didn't stop at all
Illuminating every little emotion with a haul.
As long as I drifted away from its embrace
It kept on growing in mase.

Silly me! Unaware of the molecular reaction
Taking place in the mind's perception.
The tinkling drizzle knew it.
Knock knock knock!
The composed spirit knew it.
Knock knock knock!
But the physical anatomy was still away from it.

This time I drifted away from its embrace
The drizzle sang the songs of its praise.
My spirit came forward to catch it with grace
My head hurts as I drifted away from its
embrace.
The engaging songs of the air filling the space.

Enlightening me to accept the grace
With an embrace.
I no longer juggle in mind's veil
Acceding all that is with tranquil
I surrender to my soul!
In that very moment, there is just peace that
prevails.

Love and Light

As I sat near the waves,
Under the moonlit sky
The storms within me that crave
To dissolve in that sigh.

The tsunamic waves made sense
As they depicted my inner rumpus
I carried the love with grace
My inner turmoil testing my endurance
My little heart pining for your presence.

But you are long gone!
Like the shooting star!
I just witnessed.
Like the waves that made me wet
But you are long gone!
I'm still here.

Carrying this love with grace
Testing my mind's endurance
I'm witnessing the moon
With the sounds of waves
All the love I have for you
I'm sending to the universe.
Perhaps it'll reach you

And the continuous arrival of these emotions
On my mind
For something that happened beyond
I'll see you someday again
That day waves will meet the rain
As I carry this love with grace.

Now I'm sending this love with an embrace
It's just a moment of thoughts.
As I'm sitting near the waves
Enjoying the beauty of emotions
Under the moonlit sky,
Carrying all the love and light
I hope we'll meet again,
When my love will reach inner light.

Tricky Love

In the second month of the Gregorian calendar,
The fingers swiped an ambiguous mender
That's how the air passed another parable
And the streaks of emotions touched by nibble
Neurons spreading like the embedded roots
Begins with the process of catharsis

That's when the veins curb the pain
And the heartfelt it all in its membrane
That sweet little thing called love
Enthralling all possible life's curves
And giving a blurry vision of euphoria
Like always love gave her intense Gloria.

Somehow it was unknown to the mortal
That love will unlock the destiny of a new
portal.
It was a tricky secret
Until they both would unroll the spirit of the
moment.
It is the time to go through it!
It is the time to grow through it!

Among all the nerds

Among all the nerds,
In the streak of words
And speech bouncing in mind's sherds
Not believing, it could be merdes.

The very human, as he reads
Let it all release
And cleanse the streak of words
Opening the mind's sherds
And adjusting his specs among the nerds.

The very human, as he stares
Let it all clear
The crowd was listening,
The eyes through the windows kept shining,
The very human as he believed
Let it all relieved.

The streaks of words kept floating
And made the air enchanting.
Now the words echoed in the silence
Still floating around the present minds.
All humans as they conceive thoughts
The silence ended with a round of applause.
The crowd enjoying the cluster of words

And the very human kept smiling
Among all the nerds,
The eyes through the windows kept dazzling.

I Have Found Myself

I am the purple sky,
With different shades of moon
Under the clouds if you pry
In the solid streaks of light,
Pierce through the upper crust.

My body sinking into the ocean of infinity,
Trying to touch my soul's lane.
Summer sun was ready to shine brighter for me
Autumn leaves were ready to embrace me.

But it was your love
It was like rain
I was fully drenched.

The rain embraced me and I was floating in love
All around me.
Every ounce of my breath was drenched
An enigma of love
All around me.

Words coming to me automatically
My soul drenched in love
The air and the aroma of soil embraced me
I could see your soul through your eyes

Like the vast sea.

I have found myself ,
I am the purple sky,
With different shades of moon
Under the clouds, if you pry.